BREADCRUMBS AND BURNING BUSHES:

Tracing God's Clues and Encounters

By

Dr. Tarasha Lloyd

ISBN: 979-8-218-79599-3

Scripture Notice:

Published by Lloyd Consulting Company, PLLC. Printed in the United States of America

Dedication

To my Abba (my father), and to my Sasha—the one I follow, and the one who walks beside me...

To my sister circle, my sisters in Christ—thank you for walking with me, praying with me, and standing as wise counselors on this journey (You know who you are).

Sherry—thank you for affirming my spiritual identity in the hidden place. During the quiet process of refinement, where God was developing my gifts and character like a photograph in a darkroom—slowly, intentionally, and beautifully—you saw me.

Countless times, I called you in the early morning hours (before you were even fully awake), starting with the words, "I had a dream." And every time, you listened. Thank you for being a spiritual covering and a safe space to speak what many might never understand.

Through the wisdom, presence, and unwavering truth of each of you, I've emerged clearer, stronger, and more deeply rooted in Him.

Forever grateful

Contents

Dedication...iii

Introduction 1

Day1: Presence over Perfection: A Personal Parable from God 3

Day 2: When God sets the Table (Let him Cook) 7

Day 3: Meeting in the Mess: The importance of grace 10

Day 4: Leftovers and Letting go 13

Day 5: Lessons from the Bummer Lamb: On heartbreak and other hard stuff 16

Day 6: Gratitude: The Quiet Power 20

Day 7: The Book of Remembrance 23

Selah: Week 1 (Pause and Reflect)...27

Day 8: Finish Well: A Track Revelation 28

Day 9: Giants Fall: When God Makes a Way 31

Day 10: Imposter, Interrupted 34

Day 11: When God takes the Training Wheels off.......................................37

Day 12: Promise meets Process: The undoing 40

Day 13: Let it Rain..43

Day 14: Full Speed Ahead! 46

Selah: Week 2 (Rest and Renewal)...49

Day 15: The Pop that Saved me: A lesson on God's Correction 50

Day 16: When God makes you Shine (The Moses glow) 53

Day 17: The Flight of Obedience 57

Day 18: From Bondage to Bread (Daily Bread) 60

Day19: A Table for the Weary: The day God spoke out loud 64

Day 20: Stay on the Wall! (How Focus Protects your Purpose)...................68

Day 21: Faith like Christmas Morning (The Big Red Box) 72

Selah: Week 3 (Abide and Prepare) 75

Bonus: The Listening Room (7 keys to hearing God's voice) 76

He Speaks in many ways (Overview) 77

Key 1: The Word of God — His Voice in Scripture 79

Key 2- The Whispering place: The art of stillness 82

Key 3: Dreams and Visions: Night parables and divine downloads 84

Key 4: Patterns, Repetitions and Clues: When he confirms 87

Key 5: Silence Isn't Absence: Hearing in Quiet Seasons 89

Key 6: Godly Counsel & Prophetic words: Using others Wisely 91

Key 7: Peace vs. Pressure: God doesn't Manipulate 94

The Ongoing Conversation (Closing note) 96

About the Author 97

Introduction

God speaks to me through prophetic dreams and visions—and has done so since I was 9 years old. I saw a lot that I did not understand at first. Some things even frightened me. But through intentional consecration and spiritual growth, I've learned how to better discern and decode the messages he shares with me.

This devotional is the fruit of a 40-day fast. During that time, God nudged me repeatedly to begin writing again—even sending people (unaware to them) to remind me it was time to release my second book.

What you hold in your hands is a detailed look at my journey with Christ: how he speaks, how he leads, and the personal parables and lessons he's used to shape my life. **Breadcrumbs** are the small, somewhat ordinary signs that God leaves along your path to guide you, while **burning bushes** are more obvious, undeniable holy encounters where the voice of God is unmistakably clear.

Each daily entry includes:

- A spiritual lesson or reflection

- A song of the day

- Relevant scripture(s)

- Reflective prompt(s) to help you engage more deeply in your own walk with God.

The songs listed are worship tracks that came to mind as I wrote each entry. I encourage you to take a moment to listen to them; they're part of the experience.

At the end of each week, you'll find a section titled "Selah"—a weekly wrap-up and invitation to pause. In Scripture, *Selah* often signals a moment to reflect, to breathe, and to sit with what's been spoken. This section will offer space to help you anchor the week's lessons in your life.

Finally, at the end of this book are seven extra lessons/keys that place detailed focus on helping each reader understand how to hear God speak to them personally.

My hope is that this devotional helps you see God as a loving Father—one who is always willing and ready to guide you in your daily life. And that as you read, you'll begin to recognize how he speaks to *you* personally, right where you are.

Day 1

Presence over Perfection: A Personal Parable from God

I had a dream recently where a man I know in waking life asked me a question... **"are you the perfect woman or the giving woman?"** Before I could speak the truth, I caught myself about saying the one thing I thought would make me more acceptable. Then, I paused and briefly reflected. What came out of my mouth was *truth*.

I said, "I'm the giving woman."

From the conversation, a personal parable between the Lord and I was born. Upon awakening, I understood the lesson in totality. The perfect woman is performance based. She must have it all and do it all right, no mistakes. As a result, she is exhausted.

But the giving woman, she is different. The giving woman offers herself from a place of fullness. Think **overflow.**

She doesn't love to earn approval, but she gives because its who she is.

That moment in the dream—so simple—taught me something lasting.

We are trained to believe that being perfect earns us love. But the kingdom honors presence over perfection.

Jesus doesn't come close when we perform. He draws near when we're honest, when we give who we are, not what we think others want.

I was reminded of the story of two sisters, Martha and Mary in the bible. Jesus was visiting the home of the sisters, and their approach during his time there was vastly different. Martha stayed busy.

Preparing, hosting and becoming frantic as she worked to do everything right.

Mary, on the other hand, sat at the feet of Jesus, treasuring his presence. It wasn't passive, it was present. And Jesus called it the better choice.

Perfection doesn't matter.

But presence does

Love does and,

Wholeness does

So, if you are striving, let today be the day that you lay down what you were never called to do, which was earn what God already made yours. You were designed to love deeply, give fully, and rest in the truth that real love never asks for perfection.

And in my dream, when I stopped trying to say the "right thing" and simply said the *real thing*, love didn't back away. It leaned in.

Scripture:

> *"Martha, Martha," the Lord answered, "you are worried and upset about many things, but few things are needed—or indeed only one. Mary has chosen what is better, and it will not be taken away from her."*
>
> **Luke 10:41–42 (NIV)**

Song of the day: "Nothing Else" Cody Carnes

Reflective prompts:

When have I chosen performance or perfection over simply being present with God or others? Why?

What does it look like for me, practically, to choose the "better thing" in this season?

Notes

Day 2

When God sets the Table
(Let him Cook)

In February of 2020, just before the Covid-19 lockdowns and widespread pandemonium began, I had the privilege of taking a cruise. I joined a few of my Doctoral cohorts for some sun and fun. Boarding a plane to Galveston, Texas, for the inaugural *Doctors at Sea* cruise, I was excited about the prospect of taking a pause from all my busyness to focus on rest.

Prior to boarding, I had given dietary preferences and checked them twice. Eager to see what the chefs had in store for the venturing vegans, I made my way to the dining room at dinner on the first night. But my culinary daydreams came to a screeching halt. I was told that there were **no vegan options** outside of salad for the first night (If you know me, those words are downright offensive).

With this news, I ventured back to my cabin and was startled by my room phone ringing just as I settled in. The Maître' D had confirmed that the main Chef would be in contact with me the next day. Instead, he reached out earlier than expected. He introduced himself and took the time to ask questions about my likes and dislikes. But everything he named, I **loved.**

I told him he had free reign to create whatever meals he wanted. It just so happens; he specialized in vegan/plant-based cuisine in culinary arts school and had an avid interest in creating these meals. I could hear his excitement when I granted him permission… "Surprise me" I said. And that, he did.

On that night, the chef (the one with authority in the kitchen and creative power) wanted to know my heart, my palate and my "yes" and "no." And when I gave him **permission to move freely,** he showed out. My meals were curated daily with great extravagance and beauty. I dined like royalty, with many courses from breakfast to dinner. My colleagues were curious about what I would be served each night. Each day, the Maître D' came to check on me, but I had the privilege of meeting the chef personally twice, as he came out to greet me and chat briefly. On the final night of the cruise, a bottle of red wine was waiting for my entire table. A thoughtful gift from the chef himself. Though I no longer consumed alcohol, my colleagues were able to share it. The experience was something I'll remember for the rest of my life.

When you allow the chef of your soul, El Elyon (the most high God) free reign, you will be amazed at what heaven will serve up. The Lord will lavishly feed (bless) the ones he loves. But first, we must be willing to release control of the menu and watch the table.

Scripture:

> *"You prepare a table for me in the presence of my enemies. You anoint my head with oil, my cup overflows"*

Psalms 23:5

Song of the day: Fill Me Up" – *Tasha Cobbs*

Reflective prompts:

When has God "surprised" me by preparing something better than I could've planned for myself?

(Hint: unexpected blessings or divine provision.)

What areas of my life am I still trying to control the "menu"? What would it look like to give God full creative freedom?

Notes

Day 3

Meeting in the Mess: The importance of grace

I've learned that there will be seasons of our lives where God calls us to a level of service unlike seasons past. He may call us to show up in someone else's storm. It can be messy, challenging, and inconvenient, among other things, but always worth it. In our obedience and selflessness, we show the love of God to someone in need.

I can recall a recent experience of showing up in a space that was cluttered, chaotic. It was marked by mental exhaustion, transition, and unrest. Decluttering took place on a physical and emotional level, but most of all, I was present.

There's great power in presence.

Sometimes you just need to be, and through this experience, the Holy Spirit showed me...

This is grace

I consider it to be an easy thing to give grace when a person is composed, strong, and even grateful, but the true test of grace is when the sink is full of dishes, the laundry piles up, and you are met with the person not operating at their best.

As I remember being there in a time of need, the Lord gently reminded me of the many times I too was a mess, yet he loved me enough to step into my own chaos: a life that was less than presentable an exhausted heart, a weary mind.

I felt that I had nothing polished to give him, and he never pulled away, only drew near.

Grace doesn't rush in to sanitize the scene. Grace enters with meals for the hungry and encouragement for the weary. It bends low with a towel, not to shame, but to serve. It loves without recognition or repayment.

Grace steps into the mess and never keeps score. It simply says, **"there's no charge."**

Song of the day: "No Charge" Shirley Caesar

Scripture:

> *"Now that I your Lord and teacher have washed your feet, you also should wash one another's feet. I have set you an example that you should do as I have done for you"*

John 13:14-15

Reflective Prompts:

Think about a time when someone extended grace to you in your "mess." How did their presence impact you?

Who in your life might need you to show up for them—not with answers, but simply with presence?

Notes

Day 4

Leftovers and Letting go

One of the most arduous chores for me is cleaning my refrigerator. It's something that, when done in small spurts on a regular basis, is much easier to manage. But life happens, things get busy, and I forget. The leftovers, expired snacks, and takeout containers pile up.

I admit—having a clean fridge evokes an odd sense of satisfaction for me. Seeing empty shelves, space for new things, everything freshly wiped down and sparkling—it leaves me with a lingering sense of accomplishment.

As I cleaned out my refrigerator recently, God began to minister to me about the process of creating space for the *new*.

Sometimes we hold on to things—relationships, habits, mindsets— that have long exceeded their expiration date. And while they may have once served a purpose, now they're just *taking up space*. Not only do they block what God is trying to bring into our lives— new people, new opportunities, fresh clarity—but left too long, they become hazardous.

Some things don't just get old. They *rot*. They begin to smell. They quietly release the stench of disappointment, fear, guilt, or pride— and over time, they begin to affect the entire atmosphere.

I hope you hear what I'm saying.

Clean your fridge.

Scriptures:

"And no one pours new wine into old wineskins. Otherwise, the new wine will burst the skins; the wine will run out and the wineskins will be ruined. [38] No, new wine must be poured into new wineskins."

Luke 5:37-38

"Forget the former things; do not dwell on the past. See, I am doing a new thing! Now it springs up; do you not perceive it? I am making a way in the wilderness and streams in the wasteland."

Isaiah 43:18-19

Song of the day: "New Wine" Todd Galberth ft. Chandler Moore

Reflective prompts:

What in my life feels like it's "expired"—something that once served a purpose, but now feels stagnant, draining, or misaligned?

Where is God asking me to make room—emotionally, spiritually, or even physically—for something new? How can I respond today?

Notes

$Day\ 5$

Lessons from the Bummer Lamb:
On heartbreak and other hard stuff

Recently in my quiet time, I learned about the bummer lamb.
Disclaimer: Farm animals are far outside of my area of knowledge. Therefore, it took some research and sitting with God to fully understand this lesson.

A bummer lamb is one that is rejected by its mother after birth.

This can be for a variety of reasons. I've read that it may be because of the pain of the labor associated with the lamb, or even the ewe (which is the mother sheep) being unable to feed the lamb due to things like mastitis. This causes the lamb to be rejected permanently...

It can often be seen walking around with its head hung extremely low...

The physical manifestation of being sad.

The lamb's spirit is **broken** by this of course...

They could potentially die of hunger and of course a broken spirit.

It's serious...

I know you're wondering where this is going... Stay with me...

A good shepherd is aware of the bummer lambs in their flock.

Without their intervention, the lambs wouldn't survive.

The shepherd takes these lambs personally and nurtures them.

They hold them close to their heart, allowing them to be connected and feel safe through the sound of their heartbeat.

They bottle feed them

Engulf them with love

When they grow into sheep and have been released back to the flock, the bummer sheep are the first to recognize and return to the shepherd.

They aren't more special than the others; They just have such an *intimate connection.*

They recognize the voice of the shepherd in an instant.

(I hope you're catching my drift by now)

So, I heard the question so clearly in my spirit this morning

"Tarasha, how can you relate to the bummer lamb?"

And of course, the waterworks began… (*insert ugly cry*)

The times I felt so ***brokenhearted*** I could barely get out of bed

I felt I might succumb to ***grief***

I felt ***lost*** and had so many ***questions*** about life and purpose

It was in those times that the ***good shepherd*** nursed me back to health.

Gave me ***strength, vitality***

and ***understanding*** my purpose on earth.

I can most definitely relate to the bummer lamb.

Can you?

Whether it was your actual mother, a lover or any other person that you leaned on for love or support, I invite you to seek God, the good shepherd, who is more than able to take the hurt, rejection and broken heart and replace it with love, nurturing and support.

Scriptures:

"He heals the brokenhearted and binds up their wounds

"You've kept track of all my wandering and my weeping. You've stored my many tears in your bottle- not one will be lost. For they are all recorded in your book of remembrance"

Psalms 56:8 TPT

Song of the day: Alabaster Box- Cece Winans

Reflective prompt:

Can I identify a season or experience in my life when I felt rejected, abandoned, or unseen—like the bummer lamb? How did that impact my heart, and where do I still need healing?

(Take a moment to reflect on a wound that may still be lingering— and invite God into that space.)

Bonus prompt:

Now that I've experienced the Shepherd's healing, how might He be calling me to recognize and care for other "bummer lambs" in my own life—those who feel rejected, overlooked, or brokenhearted?

(Ask God to reveal someone who may need the same love and tenderness you once received.)

Notes

Day 6

Gratitude: The Quiet Power

The days are swiftly passing by. As the months fly by quickly, I encourage you to find a quiet moment to reflect on your life.

What is it that you hope to become?

It's so easy to get caught in the relentless hustle the laundry the dishes homework meetings chauffeuring kids to practice after practice (if you have school-aged children, can I get an amen?)—that we lose sight of who we are becoming beneath all the doing.

Yes, we must do the work of life, but we also need to sit at the feet of our Father, reflect on our journey, dream about where we want to go, and above all, express gratitude.

I once read that "Gratitude is what turns an ordinary day into a holiday," and I couldn't agree more.

These days, I carry the joy of the Lord in my heart, unbothered by obstacles that once would have tripped me up. Want to know the secret? Gratitude.

Taking time each day to thank God for the gift of waking up—before my feet even touch the ground—helps me remember those I have lost and cherish the simple blessing of a new day.

Gratitude has the power to transform sadness into gladness and open doors I never imagined were waiting for me.

I invite you to try it.

Each day, write down or recite three things you are grateful for, big or small. There's no right or wrong answer; every win counts.

Scripture:

*"Rejoice always, pray continually, give thanks in all circumstances;
for this is God's will for you in Christ Jesus"*

1 Thessalonians 5:16-18

Song of the day: "I'll always be Thankful" Duranice Pace and
the Pace family

Reflective Prompts:

What are three things I am grateful for today?

How can cultivating gratitude shift my perspective in moments of
struggle or stress?

Notes

Day 7

The Book of Remembrance

In a recent dream, I was sitting in a circle with women I didn't know and a prophetic voice I did. It was a women's event. We began to pass around a book—its pages filled only with illustrations, almost like a graphic novel or children's book. No words, yet every image spoke volumes.

The first time the book was passed around clockwise. When it was my turn, the book landed on two pages that I read and reviewed. They were desires of my heart and things that God promised me. I quickly realized, this was a book about our destinies. As the book went around the group, I continued to observe.

Later, we passed it counterclockwise. I knew by counting the women before me that I would land on the same pages again. I had already claimed what was on them.

While chatting with the lady next to me, I looked up to see the prophet—sitting right beside me—reading my pages. She then handed me the book, but before I could read, she stopped me and rebuked me for not paying attention, because she had already read them.

I was livid.

I understood the seriousness of the book.

But when I woke and sat with God, His voice was clear:

What God has for me will be for me

I won't miss it

It can't be taken

It can't be exchanged

Its mine…

God immediately reminded me of the book of Esther.

On one night, the King could not sleep and bought in the book of records/remembrance.

In the book, it had been written that Mordecai (Esther's uncle) uncovered a plot to assassinate the King. Despite him literally fighting for his life and the lives of the Jewish people, Mordecai was honored.

Nothing could stop what God had planned and ordained for his life.

His obedience and loyalty were rewarded

And eventually, due to he and Esthers's obedience to God, the Jewish people were saved.

So, if you are ever discouraged about something not working out the way you felt it should

If you feel like it's too late

Or maybe you missed out on something big

Know that the pages of your life are still turning, and God is the ultimate author.

And the ink of his promises never fades.

Scripture: Esther 6:1-14

Song of the Day: "It is for me" Miami Mass Choir

Reflective Prompts:

Like Mordecai, how can you remain faithful in seasons when your obedience isn't yet being rewarded?

If you could "pass the book" to someone else, what testimony or truth would you want your pages to declare about God's faithfulness?

Notes

Selah: Week 1 *(Pause and Reflect)*

Take a moment to pause and remember.

What stood out to you this week?

Where did you sense God's presence most strongly?

What truth do you need to hold onto?

Write, pray, or simply sit with God in this moment of stillness.

Day 8

Finish Well: A Track Revelation

On a sunny Saturday, I was at my daughter's track meet. It was a sweltering 92-degree day in the south. For the 11 hours that I supported her, I spent about 95% of the time under the tents her coach so graciously provided. For a brief period, I emerged from the tent to venture to the bottom of the bleachers and observe to 4x100 relays. These have always been my favorite part of the meets.

Shortly before my daughter and her teammates were up, I watched the younger athletes assemble their teams. During the 7–8-yearold girls' race, I witnessed a little girl who appeared frightened at first. Before I knew it, she took off as fast as her little legs could carry her. As she ran, suddenly, she began to slow down and look back, scanning the bleachers for her dad. It was then that her father yelled as loud as he could "KEEP RUNNING! DON'T LOOK BACK!" The little girl took off again at full speed.

Though she peeked over her shoulder once more, she quickly realized there was no need. Her father's voice echoed loudly

"KEEP RUNNING, DON'T STOP! KEEP GOING!"

And that she did.

Right through the finish line, coming in at second place.

Had she not paused to look back, I am confident she would have remained in first place. I took the moment in and Abba (father) as he always does, began to speak.

No matter what happens in life, we must run on with the voice of our heavenly father as our guide. Just like the little girl, who recognized her dad's voice over everyone else cheering in the stadium, it is vital that we recognize when (and how) he speaks to us. And when we do, there is no looking back.

Finish your race and finish strong

God will lead you on to victory, if only you heed his voice.

Scripture:

> *"Whether you turn to the right or to the left, your ears will hear a voice behind you saying 'this is the way; walk in it"*

Isaiah 30:21 (NIV)

Song of the day: "You know my name" Tasha Cobbs Leonard

Reflective prompts:

What causes you to 'look back' in your own race? How can you anchor your focus on the father's voice instead?

Bonus Reflection:

"How well do you recognize the sound of God's voice? What practices help you hear Him more clearly?

Notes

Day 9

Giants Fall:
When God Makes a Way

I recently met an older gentleman in Walmart and our conversation ended up on the goodness of God. As we sat, waiting for our cars to be serviced, it was refreshing to reflect on ways God had made for us when we least expected it. As I drove off, I was also reminded of the obstacles, the mocking voices/nay sayers during those times. You see, when God tells me something, I stand on it with **everything in me.** When I have a goal, no one can tell me I won't meet it. But that doesn't mean my journey has been absent of the doubters, the mockers and those who question "is God really with her?" But every time, **God came through.**

One story I shared in conversation was when I purchased my first home as a single woman. You see, there was a particular neighborhood I had my sights set on. There were also specific desires I had for the house itself. I was told I was asking for too much on many occasions, among other things. But that didn't discourage me. Long story short, not only did I get the house in the neighborhood I wanted and with the things I desired, but I got way more than I originally asked for. The house was also discounted well below my max price and at closing, I only owed $16.99.

There are so many stories I could share about the ways God has made for me. I could draft an entire book on that subject alone.

For those who put their trust in him and practice obedience, you can guarantee that God will make a way when things look impossible.

And the limitations, obstacles and mocking voices will always fall before his promises.

Scripture:

> *"Therefore know* [without any doubt] *and understand that the Lord your God, He is God, the faithful God, who is keeping His covenant and His* [steadfast] *lovingkindness to a thousand generations with those who love Him and keep His commandments"*

Deuteronomy 7:9 (AMP)

Song of the Day: "Made a Way" Travis Greene

Reflective prompts:

What promises has God spoken to me that others may have doubted or dismissed? How have I responded to those voices— both theirs and mine?

Can I recall a time when God made a way for me—against the odds, beyond what I asked or imagined? What did it teach me about His character and timing.

Notes

Day 10

Imposter, Interrupted

There have been many moments I felt God calling me to dream bigger, step deeper, go further. On the other hand, I heard another voice. Not so kind or encouraging but sent to sabotage every work before they were ever created. One that makes me question the quality and necessity of my writing. One that says:

"Who do you think you are?"

"You're not ready."

"You're not enough."

Or my personal favorite:

"There are already so many devotionals. What makes yours different?"

It's the voice of **self-doubt,** and I've wrestled with it more times than I can count. If I am being honest, God has been nudging me to write this devotional for a little over a year. I had already written one book, received multiple testimonies from readers—but still, I questioned whether I was qualified to release something deeper, more vulnerable. I wondered if people would receive it, if I was spiritually mature "enough," wise "enough," healed "enough." And in his loving kindness, he sent reminders in the form of multiple people questioning "when will you release another book?" He sent encouragement as well.

I've come to learn that **God does not call the flawless—He calls the willing.**

Self-doubt doesn't disqualify you. *Silence doesn't disqualify you. Delay doesn't disqualify you.* God can still use you—**because He called you with full knowledge of your insecurities.**

In the Bible, Moses questioned his ability to speak. Jeremiah thought he was too young. Gideon saw himself as the least. So, if you struggle with those negative internal voices like I do, understand this...

God chose them

God chose us—and He hasn't changed.

Scripture:

> *"Casting down imaginations, and every high thing that exhalteth itself against the knowledge of God, and bringing into captivity every thought to the obedience of Christ"*

2 Corinthians 10:5 (KJV)

Song of the Day: "Flaws" Kierra Sheard

Reflective prompt:

Recall a season when you felt 'not good enough.' How did that belief influence your choices, actions, or faith in that moment?

Notes

Day 11

When God takes the Training Wheels off

In my current season of preparation and refinement, God has led me to a Bible-based counselor. Similar to a therapist, but more like a mentor or sister in Christ. As we peel back the layers of big emotions and past experiences, the Lord uses her to gently lead me back to His Word. I study the scriptures she suggests with great hunger—**willing to let them shape my life, shift old mindsets, and stir deeper growth**.

In this place, I've learned so much about what God thinks of me and His intentions toward me. The more you read His Word, the more He begins to speak directly to your situation through it. You'll begin to remember past experiences or gain new clarity about your present just by sitting quietly with what you've read.

He has beautiful, surprising ways of making His lessons stick.

One of those moments came through Hosea 2:14–16.

After a session with my counselor, she closed in prayer and shared that passage with me. I was curious. I read it repeatedly—along with the entire chapter for context. The next morning in my prayer time, God prompted me to read it again. Around 6 a.m., I emailed my counselor to ask about her own personal lessons from it.

Days later, in my quiet time, God made it personal.

Hosea 2:14–16 was His way of reminding me how He had drawn me closer—into a quiet place to hear **only** His voice. How did He do this? Through my relocation.

In 2023, I moved to South Carolina with my daughter and our dog. I had no family there. No friends. Just the three of us—and God. In these two years, I've grown so much. **God took off the training wheels**, and I had to learn to ride without (physical) support for a time.

Now, friendships are emerging. Community is being built. But for a long stretch, it was just me working, writing, raising my daughter—and spending time with God. It was necessary. He used that season to help me recognize His voice above all others—even my own. He dealt with the heavy things in my heart without interference. He taught me His character, His Word, and sharpened my discernment.

During this time, I also felt called away from social media. But in His own way, God fulfilled every word of that passage in Hosea. He allured me to a quiet place—and there, He spoke tenderly to me.

That relocation—scary as it was—became a blessing. I've watched my daughter thrive and, in her own way, remove her training wheels too. Our relationship has deepened in ways that can only be described as sacred. Even our dog responds to the peace in our home.

Sometimes, the most fruitful seasons begin in unfamiliar soil—where God has your full attention. He speaks the clearest in places where nothing else competes.

Scriptures: Hosea 2:14-16
Song of the Day: "Most Beautiful/So in Love" Maverick City

Reflective prompt:

What "training wheels" might God be asking you to let go of in this season? What fears or hopes come up when you think about it?

Notes

Day 12

Promise meets Process: The undoing

In this sacred season, God has been teaching me something tender yet powerful: I am not required to prepare for the next chapter of my life entirely alone. While much of my growth has happened in solitude—just me and the Lord, there are aspects of preparation that are meant to be shared. There is help appointed for the journey.

Contrary to what I've absorbed in some religious environments, I am not required to have completed all the work before I step into the next season. Some parts of the process require an extra set of hands—and a softened heart willing to receive them.

During a recent devotional time, the Holy Spirit led me to reflect on two dreams he had given me. In both, I found myself in the middle of an "undoing" and an "untangling." In one dream, I was working with ropes. The first rope was short and insufficient. The second was longer—but tangled with other cords. I wasn't alone in sorting through the knots. Help arrived, and I received it. In the other dream, someone was preparing my hair. I had begun the task myself, but there wasn't enough time to finish alone. Again, help was assigned.

As I cross-referenced these dreams in prayer, the symbolism became clear: while the transitions ahead require readiness, they do not demand perfection. God is not asking for a completed project—but a surrendered heart. Taking it a step further, I realized, I was never meant to do it all alone.

Yes, God was present in the process—but so was someone else. Someone He allowed to come alongside me and contribute to my preparation. While the symbolism speaks personally to marital partnership, the deeper revelation is this: purposeful connection will often require vulnerability.

It takes humility not only to help untangle someone else—but also to be willing to be helped.

This was a significant shift in my thinking. I had long believed that I needed to be whole, healed, and perfectly prepared before God's promises could find me. But I'm learning to let go of that lie.

I don't have to be a "finished product" to be loved, seen, or joined.

There is beauty in the middle—in the unraveling, in the detangling, in the becoming. And it is there, in the holy tension of process and promise, that partnership is born.

Sometimes the becoming is the very place where love begins...

Scripture:

> *"Two are better than one, because they have a good return for their labor. If either of them falls down, one can help the other up."*

Ecclesiastes 4:9-10

Song of the Day: "Hold on, help is on the way" Whitney Houston
(From "The Preacher's Wife" soundtrack)

Reflective Prompts:

In what areas of your life have you assumed that preparation must be done alone?

Who has God gently brought into your life as a helper during a season of change?

Notes

Day 13

Let it Rain

If you know me, you know I'm a lover of nature. I love hiking. I love the beach. But above all, I love experiencing the shift of seasons. There's something about each one that stirs something deep in me.

Spring brings fresh blooms, sweet scents, and the renewal of life. **Summer** offers long, sunny days, time with my daughter, and moments full of celebration.

Autumn arrives with its vibrant foliage and crisp, quiet mornings. And **winter**—my favorite—wraps me in cozy holidays, cooler weather, and sometimes, snow.

But perhaps most surprisingly, I've also grown to love the rain. No matter the season, there's something about it that feels sacred to me now. I love the scent of the earth just after it falls, how the air feels cleaner, the world quieter. I often find myself taking my dog for a walk just to soak it in. It's like the earth exhales and everything becomes still. If I'm not outside on my rocking chair during a downpour, I'm likely curled under a blanket, soothed by its rhythm. And yes—as strange as it sounds—I even enjoy driving in it. Fewer crowds. A slower pace. A sort of peace.

I wasn't always this way. I used to retreat quickly at the first drop, unsettled by the sound of thunder and irritated by the interruption to my plans. But somewhere along the way, I stopped hiding from the rain.

I started living in it—and eventually, I learned to enjoy it.

Because life brings its own rainy seasons: a loss, a breakup, an unexpected transition, the fading of a friendship.

At first, these storms can feel inconvenient, even overwhelming. But the more I've walked with God, the more I've come to see— **rain is never wasted**.

It cleanses.

It softens.

It prepares the ground for something new.

So now, when life rains, I no longer panic or run.

I pause.

I breathe.

Sometimes, I even dance in it.

Because no matter how long it rains, it won't last forever... Sooner or later, the sun returns.

Scripture: James 1:2-4

Song of the day: "I told the storm" Greg O'Quinn and Joyful Noyze

Reflective prompts:

What beauty or growth has come from a storm I once feared?

Am I learning to find peace in the process, or am I still waiting for the sun to feel safe?

Notes

Day 14

Full Speed Ahead!

In December 2024, I joined a few girlfriends on Zoom for a vision board session. We used Canva to gather and display our visions for 2025, then shared what we created. I remember starting with a rough draft, but as I sat with God in prayer later that evening, everything shifted.

Though I'm a dreamer, I often receive visions while praying in the Spirit. Sometimes it's a flash of a person or a vivid image. Most often, I see words—suspended in the air like whispers etched in light. That night, one phrase stood out above all the rest: **"FULL SPEED AHEAD."**

Not only did I see the words, but I also saw a train blazing down the tracks at high speed. I immediately knew what God was saying.

I've learned that the wait for God's promises can feel long. He is intentional in how he aligns timing, people, and circumstances. Waiting isn't easy, especially when the desire is deep. But in the waiting, God stretches patience, builds faith, and restores our hope and trust in Him. And when the moment comes for fulfillment, **it comes with speed.**

What once felt delayed is suddenly accelerated. What looked like silence bursts into movement. The beauty of it is this: **God redeems time.** He restores what we thought was lost and causes things to unfold so swiftly, it often feels like we barely had time to process before the next breakthrough arrives.

So, whatever you're waiting on—

☛ Healing

- Financial provision
- A new job or opportunity
- Love
- Or simply an answer from God—

Don't lose sight of His promises. And above all, don't lose faith in **who he is.**

The wait is not meant to punish but to **prepare**—to grow your spiritual muscles and deepen your intimacy with Him. I can say with confidence: the wait was worth it. I've thanked God many times, not just for what He gave me, but for who I became while I waited.

So, I say, hold your vision close, and your faith even closer. When it's time, it will come—**full speed ahead.**

Scriptures:

> *"I foretold the former things long ago, my mouth announced them, and I made them known; then suddenly I acted, and they came to pass"*
>
> **Isaiah 48:3 (NIV)**

> *"I will repay you for the years the locusts have eaten- the great locust and the young locust, the other locusts and the locust swarm- my great army that I sent among you"*
>
> **Joel 2:25 (NIV)**

Song of the day: "Wait on the Lord" James Wilson feat. Brooke Staten

Reflective prompts:

What are you currently waiting on, and how is God using this season to build your faith?

Can you look back on a delay that now feels like a blessing?

Notes

Selah: Week 2

(Rest and Renewal)

Take a moment to pause and remember.

What stood out to you this week?

Where did you sense God's presence most strongly?

What truth do you need to hold onto?

Write, pray, or simply sit with God in this moment of stillness.

The Pop that Saved me:
A lesson on God's Correction

When I was a young girl, I recall being fascinated by the stovetop. Something about the orange light radiating from each eye of the stove when it was heated drew me in. (It's funny the random things you recall from childhood).

One day while spending time with my paternal grandparents, I was in the kitchen with my grandmother. I was so intrigued by the stove on that day, I decided to try to reach out and touch it. After mustering up the courage to touch something I was sure I was not supposed to touch (unbeknownst of the pain it would cause), I leaned in. My grandmother, who had a close eye on me the entire time, intercepted before my hand made contact. And my hand was met with a swift, hard tap from her.

Maybe I remember because this was the only time she ever popped me.

Maybe the experience startled me

But I remember clearly...

And in my recent reflections with God, this memory came rushing back into my mind.

As the loving father he is, God chastises those he loves.

I remember days of crying during my prayer time because things weren't going my way. Feeling heavy and discouraged, I took it to God in prayer. Whether it was a failed relationship, a missed opportunity, or something else I thought I wanted at the time, I am so thankful that like my grandmother, he stepped in right on time and blocked me from reaching things that were not meant for me. He has saved me from decisions that could have negatively impacted me for the duration of my life.

Whether it was a clear "no"

Lack of peace

A deep sense of conviction

God has always dealt with me about the choices I make and the path I take. And if you're listening, as a child of God, he is doing the same for you.

So often, we don't realize what God is protecting us from until much later—if ever. But his correction is never punishment for punishment's sake. It's redirection born out of love.

Like my grandmother's swift pop on the hand, God's intervention is not to harm us, but to keep us from harm. His "no" is sometimes the most powerful "yes" to His perfect plan. May we learn to trust even his discipline, knowing it is a mark of his deep affection and care.

Scripture: Proverbs 3:11-12

Song of the day: "Refiner" Maverick City Music & Chandler Moore feat. Steffany Gretzinger

Reflective prompt:

Think back to a time when something didn't go your way — maybe it felt like rejection, redirection, or even a "pop" from God. But now, looking back, you can see his hand in it.

Write about what happened.
What are some of the hidden blessings that emerged from that moment?
What can you thank God for now that you couldn't see then?

Notes

Day 16

When God makes you Shine
(The Moses glow)

One of the most freeing truths I've discovered in walking with God is this:

He cares about everything that concerns me.

Not just the big, spiritual matters, but also the trivial details that weigh on my heart.

Somewhere along the way, religion taught many of us that certain prayers are too small for God — as though he has more important matters to handle. But the Word says otherwise: *"Cast all your cares on Him, because He cares for you"* (1 Peter 5:7).

All means all.

We think "God wouldn't be troubled with_____" (Fill in the blank. I am sure something came to mind when you read this).

But you'd be amazed at how he honors these types of prayers, even if you don't say them aloud.

Recently, in a quiet journaling moment, I found myself wrestling with thoughts of being unpretty, feeling unmotivated, and stuck (mentally/spiritually). For a few reasons, I wasn't feeling like my usual confident self. Every woman has likely faced a season like that, where confidence wavers and the mirror doesn't reflect what you hope to see. Instead of pretending it didn't matter, I brought it to my father in prayer.

I turned to Exodus 34, where Moses came down from Mount Sinai after meeting with God. The text says his face was radiant because he had been in God's presence. The glow was so striking that others noticed it immediately.

That passage reminded me that God's presence doesn't just transform the inside — it radiates outward too.

(Pro tip: Always add scripture to your prayers).

Imagine the glory of God resting on you so powerfully that it radiated from the inside out in such a manner that it was noticeable by everyone you encountered.

In this season, God has been giving me both spiritual **and** practical instructions — about my health, my habits, even my diet, (in addition to time in his presence each day) to increase that Moses glow. Some things seem small at first glance but ultimately carry weight in how I steward my body, mind and spirit.

His love extends to those details because he wants his children to thrive wholly: body, soul, **and** spirit.

To some, this may sound unusual. But for those who have walked closely with him, it's no surprise. God is a Father who cares not only about eternal matters but also about how you feel when you look in the mirror. His presence restores radiance, and his care covers the trivial things we thought were too insignificant to bring before him.

Never hesitate to bring your "small" prayers to God — because nothing about you is small to him.

Scriptures:

> *"Gaze upon hum, join your life with his, and joy will come. Your faces will glisten with glory. You'll never wear that shame face again."*

Psalms 34:5 (TPT)

Exodus 34: 29-35

Song of the day: "Detail" Jonathan McReynolds

Reflective prompt:

If you could believe wholeheartedly that God cares about the details of your life, how would it change the way you approach your daily routines?

Notes

Day 17

The Flight of Obedience

In a recent dream, I was scheduled to check out of a hotel with friends and catch a flight home. I thought the flight was at 1 pm. As I scrambled to pack, I realized I had far more clothes and bags than before. My friends finished quickly, packed some of my essentials for me, and left ahead of me. I insisted I would catch up.

I remember leaving one huge suitcase crammed with old clothing at the hotel. I had decided that I no longer needed its contents and left it, thinking maybe someone else may need the contents.

On the way to the airport, I encountered obstacle after obstacle. I was anxious, frustrated, and convinced I had missed my flight. Yet, I pressed forward, determined to find another way. In my mind, either I was going to get there and realize the flight had been delayed, or there would be a later flight to book. Eventually, I reunited with my friends on a shuttle.

It was there that I learned three important truths:

They had kept the items I truly needed

The flight wasn't at 1:00 p.m. after all—it was at 9:30 p.m.

I would arrive at my destination much sooner than I had expected.

All along, everything had been divinely orchestrated.

But one thing was pivotal: <u>I had to leave the old baggage behind.</u>

This dream mirrored my current season. God has been calling me to release many things—old hurts and offenses, and sometimes old ways of thinking.

In the next season of your life, He may call you to do the same.

Like me, you may face tests of obedience—whether it's blessing those who curse you, serving those who misuse you, or giving away something you thought you still needed

In this season, I have been stretched me in ways I never imagined.

When he sends the next test, it is my prayer that you obey.

Your obedience will unlock more than what you've been waiting for or praying for. It opens the door to blessings you could have never imagined.

Don't be afraid to leave behind what no longer serves you. Your obedience is your boarding pass.

Will you pass the test?

Scripture:

> *"But Samuel replied: 'Does the Lord delight in burnt offerings and sacrifices as much as in obeying the Lord? To obey is better than sacrifice, and to heed is better than the fat of rams.'"*

1 Samuel 15:22 (NIV)

Song of the day: "Moving Forward" Israel Houghton

(One of my daughter's favorites)

Reflective prompt:

Have you ever thought you "missed" something in life, only to realize later that God's timing was different than yours? What did you learn?

Notes

Day 18

From Bondage to Bread
(Daily Bread)

Have you ever found yourself in a situation where you knew the only way you would make it was by God's hand? In that moment, you were out of options or ways you could think of in your own strength to resolve the issue. As a result, you found yourself in prayer, seeking God for the thing you needed.

I have experienced a few times like this that God used to build total dependence on him. I had to shut out the noise of others' opinions and dig deep to hear him clearly. In those times, he called me away from people and out of the public eye.

Not only did he answer the prayers (often in a way that exceeded what I expected or asked for), but I grew in my own personal knowledge of the heart and character of God. He really does hear the cries (of the obedient), and he answers.

If you have a good relationship with your earthly father, imagine the character of your dad times 1,000. God is more loving, compassionate, kind and responsive than mere words can describe.

There were times that I felt like the Israelites after exiting Egypt.

Particularly after relocating.

True story- God told me to pack up my home and begin releasing items I did not need about 6 months before the actual move took place.

And guess what… I had no clue where I was going.

I had a place in mind, but it turns out, he had something else in store. In obedience, I quietly began to acquire boxes, pack up my daughter and my things and make multiple trips to Goodwill.

Crazy faith, right? Along the way, there were challenges.

But there were also blessings.

There are times in my life where I have had to literally wait like the Israelites for my manna. The daily bread.

Whether it was an open-door Provision or an answer to other issues/queries

I was trained to wait for it.

The wait can get hard. You can begin to wonder, just like the Israelites, whether the choice you made to leave behind the place, person, job, **(fill in the blank)** that you were comfortable with was the right move. Isn't it funny how bondage becomes nostalgic? The shackles begin to feel normal and even comfortable after a period. I found myself living in a place where I knew the Lord had clearly told me it was time to exit. As I stayed in this place that my daughter and I had grown accustomed to, it became a prison of sorts. Stifling my growth and stunting my potential to walk into the things God was calling me into.

Obedience is hard but so is staying stuck due to disobedience.

Choose your hard

God's provision may not arrive in bulk, but his daily bread will always be right on time.

Scripture: Exodus 16:1-11

Song of the day: "Trust in God" Elevation Worship feat. Chris Brown

Reflective prompts:

When has God asked me to move in faith without showing me the destination?

What step of obedience could God be asking me to take today, even though I do not have all the details?

Notes

Day 19

A Table for the Weary:
The day God spoke out loud

There are certain moments in life when I hear God more clearly than others. His voice is distinct, his message unmistakable. One of those times is when I'm away from my daily routine — on vacation, unplugged, or simply removed from the ordinary. In the quiet, I notice him more fully.

Late spring while on a road trip, I stopped for an overnight hotel stay along the way. Exhausted after an eight-hour drive, I prayed before bed, pouring out my recent hurt and disappointment to the Lord. Then I sank into the sheets and drifted into sleep.

That night I dreamed of a long table. A hotel room. And a familiar person. We were setting the table for children who had traveled with us.

What happened next is something rare for me. In my walk with God, I can only recall hearing his audible voice three times. But that morning, as I hovered between sleep and waking, I heard the gentle, yet authoritative voice of a man:

"I am setting a table for you in the presence of your enemies."

I jolted awake.

There was no going back to sleep. Immediately, I opened my Bible to Psalms 23 and began to study.

In that moment, I knew:

- He saw me.

- He was covering me.

- He would have the final say.

The heaviness I carried into prayer the night before lifted in the light of his voice. His direct confirmations to me always lift my spirits. It always serves as a calm reassurance that he heard me, and an answer is on the way. I have never known him not to deliver.

No matter what life throws at you, if you are walking with God, trouble will not last forever. Psalm 23 reminds us that our Shepherd leads us beside still waters, comforts us in distress, and prepares a table — abundant and overflowing — for those He loves. That table holds more than we could ever ask, think, or imagine.

Scriptures:

**Psalms 20: 1-9 (my favorite verses. I pray these whenever I am in distress and need victory)

Psalms 121:1-8

"You prepare a table for me in the presence of my enemies. You anoint my head with oil; my cup overflows."

(Psalms 23:6) NIV

"Cast your cares on the LORD and he will sustain you; he will never let the righteous be shaken."

Psalms 55:22

Song of the Day: "The Hill" Travis Greene

Reflective Prompts:

Think of a time when you felt overlooked or opposed. How did God remind you that he still sees you and covers you?

If God spoke audibly to you today, what is one thing you would long to hear him say?

Notes

Day 20

Stay on the Wall!
(How Focus Protects your Purpose)

There are seasons when God gives us assignments that are meant not only to shape us but also to bless others. Recently, I found myself struggling to stay focused on one of those assignments— this very devotional you're reading. I knew God had made it clear: this must be completed before I could move on to the next thing he had prepared. Yet, I let the cares of life distract me. I chose rest, busyness, or personal interests over obedience.

Both this book and the next project, are ordained by God to help others on their healing and faith journey. In other words, there are people waiting for me to be obedient. Even with this knowledge, I found myself struggling over the last two weeks or so to finish this book. As you can see, this is day 20 of 21, so completion was a stone's throw away.

This breadcrumb is all about how God gently convicted me in the areas of focus and obedience.

As I mentioned in earlier chapters, one of the key ways God speaks to us is using his word (scriptures). 2 Timothy 3:16 reminds us that "all scripture is God-breathed and is useful for teaching, rebuking, correcting and training in righteousness." In his love, God used his word as a reminder, through Nehemiah, who was called to rebuild the wall of Jerusalem, and of the Israelites in Haggai's time, who delayed rebuilding God's temple.

In both books of the bible, there was a work to be done that was meant to glorify God. Nehemiah was building a wall, and the Israelites were assigned the task of rebuilding the temple of God.

They had returned home from Babylonian captivity and had been there for 16 years when the Prophet Haggai came with a reminder from God- this needs to get done, like yesterday (I'm paraphrasing).

When personal matters took priority, it sent the wrong message:

"God, your presence isn't important right now."

I am guilty of sometimes prioritizing personal matters over what God has told me to do **first.** Maybe you have been as well. But I have learned that I cannot expect him to move on my prayer requests without first being obedient to the unfinished work that he asked me to do.

Whether it's a project or even setting intentional time aside for prayer and scripture reading, these are all apart of restoring his temple.

Nehemiah worked without allowing distractions to derail him. After multiple attempts from those around him who opposed the work to get him to stop what he was doing he said, "I am doing a great work, and I cannot come down."

That determination is the posture we need when carrying out God's instructions. This type of obedience opens doors to blessings.

For years, people suggested I release my first book in eBook format. I resisted—until I realized the audiobook I had a desire to produce required one. Once I obeyed, not only did the audiobook release, but God used both the eBook and audiobook to expand my reach through book signings, speaking invitations, and new opportunities I hadn't imagined.

Obedience matters. Delayed obedience is still disobedience. And disobedience can delay blessings, breakthroughs, and even the people waiting for your testimony.

As I assemble this second body of work, doors continue to open for the book I released 4 years ago. Imagine that.

We can create stagnation, or the inability to move forward, just by delaying our obedience.

If this speaks to you, I encourage you to take the time to do some personal inventory. Set boundaries where they are needed with your time to get these things done.

Your obedience may be the key that unlocks not only your breakthrough, but someone else's. Stay on the wall—your obedience is bigger than you, and your work matters more than you know.

Scriptures:

"But seek first his kingdom and his righteousness, and all these things will be given to you as well"

Matthew 6:33 (NIV)

Nehemiah 6 (in its entirety), Haggai (in its entirety),

Song of the Day: "A Great Work" Brian Courtney Willson

Reflective Prompts:

Is there an "unfinished assignment" in your life that God has asked you to complete but you've delayed? What small step can you take this week to get back on the wall?

Nehemiah declared, *"I am doing a great work, and I cannot come down."* What distractions most often tempt you to "come down" from your assignment, and how can you guard against them?

Notes

Day 21

Faith like Christmas Morning
(The Big Red Box)

A few years ago, during prayer with a sister in Christ, she shared a vision of me opening a big red box and crying tears of joy. There was an understanding that this was something I had waited and believed for over many years. And when I received it, I was overcome with joy and gratitude.

Like a child on Christmas morning, I have opened and appreciated many gifts from my father. But that *one thing*—the big red box—is still in process.

Even so, my posture continues to be just that… childlike. I carry faith that this is part of God's promises to me, and because his word is sure, I will receive it in time.

Hebrews 11:6 reminds us that "without faith it is impossible to please God, because anyone who comes to Him must believe that He exists and that He rewards those who earnestly seek Him" (NIV). Jesus also emphasizes the power of childlike faith:

> *"Truly I tell you, anyone who will not receive the kingdom of God like a little child will never enter it."* —Luke 18:17 (NIV)

Childlike faith is a higher level of trust. It believes without needing all the answers. It carries dependence, wonder, and innocence— free from pride and cynicism.

Think about it: when we were children, we believed in all kinds of things without second-guessing. Whether it was Santa, the Easter

Bunny, or simply trusting our parents to meet our needs, our hearts leaned on hope more than logic.

That same posture is vital in how we approach God. What we believe about *His nature* shapes how we wait, how we hope, and how we worship—even when the gift we long for hasn't arrived yet.

Until the big red box arrives, I'll keep showing up like a child on Christmas morning—heart full of wonder, eyes fixed on the Giver.

I hope you do the same…

Scripture:

> *"If you, then, though you are evil, know how to give good gifts to your children, how much more will your Father in heaven give good gifts to those who ask him!"*

Matthew 7:11 (NIV)

Song of the day: "Promises" Maverick City Music, Joe L Barnes and Naomi Raine

Reflective prompts:

What is my "big red box"?

(Name the promise/desire you are still waiting on)

If the promise arrived today, would I be ready to receive it with joy or would fear, doubt, or control get in the way?

Notes

Selah: Week 3
(Abide and Prepare)

Take a moment to pause and remember.

What stood out to you this week?

Where did you sense God's presence most strongly?

What truth do you need to hold onto?

Write, pray, or simply sit with God in this moment of stillness.

Bonus: The Listening Room

(7 keys to hearing God's voice)

He Speaks in many ways
(Overview)

"Then Jesus said, 'whoever has ears to hear, let them hear.'"

Mark 4:9 (NIV)

In my first book, "The Self- Love Commandments: A Woman's guide to Healing, Freedom and Love" I touched on learning to hear the voice of God briefly. This is a subject I am personally very passionate about in my walk with Christ.

For many years, prayer was a one-way conversation. I was taught to pray, but never to listen. There were many times I felt discouraged, wondering if he heard my prayers because I had no idea how to hear his response.

Then one day, I learned about the 5x5x5 challenge (5 minutes of scripture, 5 minutes of prayer and 5 minutes of sitting quietly) and my life changed forever. I learned that God is always speaking, whether we hear him or not. He doesn't stop. All day long, he is leading, guiding and instructing. Having an ear that will take the time to hear is vital.

In this section, I will talk about the methods he uses, how to discern his voice from others and how to continue growing in communication with God.

God speaks in many ways. He often uses:

- Scripture
- Dreams and Visions
- Patterns/repetition
- Godly counsel and/or Prophetic voices
- Inner witness/peace
- Circumstances

- Nature

And though rare, he can speak in his audible voice

For this section of the book, I'll talk more about dreams and visions, Godly counsel and prophetic voices and patterns/repetitions.

The voice of God may echo in dreams, whisper through peace, or thunder in confirmation—but however he speaks, he's calling you closer.

Key 1

The Word of God —
His Voice in Scripture

Scripture Anchor:

"All Scripture is God-breathed and is useful for teaching, rebuking, correcting and training in righteousness, so that the servant of God may be thoroughly equipped for every good work."

2 Timothy 3:16–17 (NIV)

Key Point: If you want to recognize God's voice, start with his word. Every other method he uses — dreams, whispers, confirmations — will **always** align with what he has already spoken in scripture.

Teaching:

You don't need a theology degree to hear God in his word. In other words, what separates you from your Pastor, Apostle, or local Prophet is the decision to walk with God (in obedience), read his word and seek him consistently (prayer). You too can hear him clearly, with time and dedication. There are so many resources that can help you in this area (I have listed some at the end of this section).

What matters is not how much you read, but how you read: slowly, prayerfully, attentively.

God's Word is alive. A verse you've read ten times may suddenly strike your heart with fresh clarity. A phrase may "leap off the page" in a way that speaks directly to your situation. That's the Spirit breathing life into the text. A verse I've read dozens of times suddenly takes on new meaning and I gain fresh perspective. This is the living nature of God's word—it meets us where we are. It shifts hearts and mindsets. It gently corrects, refines and develops its reader.

Of all the methods God uses to speak to his children, I believe his written word is the most vital. It is impossible to know God—or to recognize his voice—without first knowing his word.

I've often seen how this works when documenting dreams. Sometimes the interpretation comes right away; other times, God draws me into his word to find the meaning. Every dream given by him has roots in scripture, in one way or another. This is the anchor, the filter, and the safeguard for discerning his voice.

Pro tips:

If you struggle to understand certain bible translations, I encourage you to find one that speaks to you clearly. I often reference the King James Version, but my primary study tool is the New International Version (NIV) because personally, it's easier to grasp. Bible apps today offer a wide range of translations, and many also include audio readings and reading plans that can help build consistency.

Another tool I've found invaluable is a bible commentary, which explains the context of each chapter and helps illuminate what you're reading.

Discernment tip:

The word of God is also the **primary tool** for discernment—an anchor that helps you filter what you hear. What you hear in prayer generally comes from one of three voices:

- Your own voice (shaped by your desires, fears, or thoughts)

- The voice of the enemy (deceptive or condemning)

- The voice of God (peaceful, pure, confirming, and aligned with His word)

Reflection question:

What verse or passage has God been using to speak to you recently, and what has it revealed about His heart toward you?

Key 2

The Whispering place:
The art of stillness

Scripture Anchor:

"He says, 'Be still and know that I am God; I will be exalted among the nations, I will be exalted in the earth"

Psalms 46:10 (NIV)

Key Point: Stillness is not about inactivity but about intentional presence. In the quiet, undistracted space of your day, you become sensitive to the whisper of the Holy Spirit.

Teaching:

In a world filled with things that fight for our attention and have the potential to keep us distracted, the ability to sit in stillness is truly a lost art. Our phones, tablets, smart tv's and various apps all have the tendency to be thieves of our time and focus. Tuning out distractions to hear the voice of God requires diligence and consistency. It's a necessary practice for spiritual growth and development.

Afterall, it's impossible to know what God's will is for your life... what his instructions are, what path he wants you to take, if you can't hear what he is saying.

Begin by asking yourself:

- What's the first thing I reach for when I wake up?

- Where does my mind go when I'm bored or stressed?

- What fills the last hour of my day before sleep?

Your answers reveal both your distractions and your opportunities. Slight changes in these areas can open wide spaces for stillness with God.

Practical stillness looks different for each person. For me, it often comes in the early hours of the morning when my household is quiet, and my phone is still on "Do Not Disturb." For you, it may be during a lunch break, an evening walk, or the final minutes before bed. The time of day is less important than the intentionality you bring.

The whispering place becomes sacred ground, not because of what we do, but because of who meets us there. He is waiting—are you willing to pause and listen?

Discernment tip:

When you quiet your heart and mind, notice what surfaces. A word, a phrase, or even a gentle nudge may be God's whisper. Write it down. Don't dismiss it as "just a thought." Stillness gives him room to speak.

Reflection Question:

What time in your daily rhythm could you guard as your whispering place—a consistent pause where God has your full attention?

Key 3

Dreams and Visions: Night parables and divine downloads

Scripture Anchor:

"And afterward, I will pour out my Spirit on all people. Your sons and daughters will prophesy, your old men will dream dreams, your young men will see visions"

Joel 2:28 (NIV)

Key point: Dreams and visions are powerful ways God speaks — but they require discernment. Every dream should be tested in prayer and measured against Scripture.

Teaching:

Dreams and visions are one of God's most vivid languages, but they are also one of the most easily misunderstood. A dream may come from God, from your own thoughts and emotions, or even from the enemy. Prayerful discernment is required.

Some believe that the enemy cannot interfere with dreams. I disagree. If there are doors open in your life to things that are not of God, your dreams can serve as a playground for Satan to deceive, sow fear or confusion.

Though God can send some dreams that are not pleasant to serve as warnings, if you awaken from a dream afraid, I will caution you to pray about that dream. In my earlier years as a dreamer, I have experienced nightmares. A nightmare meant to paralyze you with fear is **not** from God.

If you are a dreamer, especially one who started dreaming at an early age, the enemy can create fear through dreams, causing you to push away from your gift. Your dream life is something that needs constant monitoring, prayer and submission to God.

If you are obedient to the heeding of God, he will use dreams and visions frequently to provide instruction/direction, warning and comfort. As you grow in this area, you'll begin to recognize rhythms in how God speaks: repeated symbols, confirmations, or connections to Scripture. I've seen God warn me of false opportunities, reveal the true intentions of people, and redirect my steps through dreams. What looks good is not always from God. Remember, sugar and salt look alike, but one sweetens and the other destroys.

Pro tip:

The word says to guard your heart. What we expose ourselves to has a way of slowly leaving an imprint on us internally, regardless of whether we are aware this is happening or not. God gently nudged me to be mindful of guarding my eyes and ears (what I watch and listen to). There was a period, I turned away from television completely and certain music was off limits. In turn, my ability to hear God speak was sharpened and without the interference of the world around me.

Discernment tip:

As with any other means of hearing from God, your dreams and visions should be in alignment with the word of God. If you have a dream or vision that goes against scripture, this is a sign that it is not from God. Prayer is needed. Do not come into agreement with the dream/vision (pray Isaiah 7:7 cast it down and rebuke it).

Reflection Question:

Have you ever had a dream that brought clarity, direction, or warning? How did you test it, and what did you learn about God's voice through it?

Key 4

Patterns, Repetitions and Clues: When he confirms

Scripture Anchor:

> *"Every matter must be established by the testimony of two or three witnesses."*

2 Corinthians 13:1 (NIV)

Key Point: God often confirms His voice through patterns, repetitions, and subtle clues — but discernment is needed to recognize what's from Him and what's not.

Teaching:

There are many stories in the bible that come to mind when I think about God repeating himself to confirm things. One of the clearest examples of divine confirmation is found in the story of Gideon (Judges 6). God called Gideon to lead Israel into battle, yet Gideon asked for repeated signs to be sure it was truly the Lord's instruction. Each time, God answered patiently, confirming His word until Gideon's faith was strengthened.

In our lives, God often works the same way. You may notice that you see something repeatedly. The same phrase from different people or encountering a song or theme again and again. Even scripture, a phrase, a title or hearing a song repeatedly, it could very well be God attempting to get your attention.

If you can connect that thing you're seeing or hearing back to your prayers, it's highly likely you are receiving a response. The trouble lies in the fact that so often these patterns or repetitions lie in things that appear ordinary. As a result, they can be easily overlooked by the untrained eye/ear.

Pro tip:

God can use *anything* to confirm His word — Scripture, nature, music, people, or even daily circumstances. Don't limit Him. Keep a journal to track recurring themes or signs. Over time, you'll begin to see how threads weave together. You will be surprised at what you discover.

Discernment tip:

Always measure patterns and repetitions against Scripture. God's confirmations will never contradict His word or lead you into sin. The enemy also counterfeits signs to mislead, so stay prayerful and rooted in truth. I cannot say this enough.

Reflection Question:

Have you noticed something repeating in your life recently — a verse, a phrase, or a theme? What might God be confirming through it?

Key 5

Silence Isn't Absence: Hearing in Quiet Seasons

Scripture Anchor:

"My God, I cry out by day, but you do not answer, by night, but I find no rest"

Psalms 22:2 (NIV)

Key Point: God's silence does not equal His absence. Often, He is shaping maturity, testing faith, or drawing us to listen in new ways.

Teaching:

There is a saying: *"The Teacher is always silent during the test."* Many of us can relate to seasons where God feels silent. Some assume this means he is distant—but Scripture tells us otherwise: *He will never leave us or forsake us.* This theme is repeated in numerous ways in scripture. This emphasizes the importance of remembering that he is always near.

Silence is not abandonment. Some may argue that he is far away, which is untrue.

Sometimes, we miss his voice because we are distracted or only listening for the answer we want or have already predetermined is the right one. At other times, his silence is intentional, designed to deepen our discernment and anchor us in wisdom.

In my own walk with God, I notice that his silence is also connected to my spiritual maturity. Earlier on in my walk, I knew he was with me. He spoke clearly and frequently. Moving quickly to provide confirmation and thus, growing my confidence in the ability to discern his voice. But as I matured, the silence grew.

This is not neglect, but strategic training. Just like a teacher trusts an older student to apply what they have learned, God trusts us to walk out what he has already spoken.

Yes, it is a test. But because he is such a loving, kind father, it's always open book.

The silence is purposeful, and it does not last forever.

And when the quiet season lifts, his gentle nudges, conviction, and clarity return. I picture it like a teacher handing back an exam, red marks included—not to shame, but to help us grow for the next lesson.

God's silence is not His absence. It is often His way of saying: *"Trust what I've already spoken and let your roots grow deeper."*

Pro tip:

If you feel you can't hear God, pause and check for interference.

Busyness, constant noise, and overstimulation create static. Sometimes a fast from social media, unnecessary conversations, or endless scrolling clears the space to hear again. Even a few days of intentional quiet can sharpen your spiritual ears.

Reflective Question:

What distractions most often compete with God's voice in your daily routine? How can you clear space to make room for Him?

Key 6

Godly Counsel & Prophetic words: Using others Wisely

Scripture Anchor:

"Dear friends, do not believe every spirit, but test the spirits to see whether they are from God, because many false prophets have gone into the world"

1 John 4:1 (NIV)

Key Point: God often speaks through people—prophets, mentors, pastors, and trusted spiritual leaders—but their words must always be tested and confirmed against his word.

Teaching:

Another area in which God speaks that can be controversial is prophecy. In the bible, God often uses Prophets to deliver messages to individuals or groups of people. These messages could be of encouragement, confirmation and even warning. You see often in the Old Testament examples of God warning groups of people (I.E.- the Israelites) to turn from their ways to avoid impending doom. Earlier in this book, I mentioned the book of Haggai, where God used a Prophet to remind the Israelites that they needed to finish building his temple or suffer consequences due to their disobedience. God speaks to his Prophets, and they have great responsibility to share what God has given them without distorting the word by taking away or adding to it.

In addition to his Prophets, God may call on other leadership or those serving in the role of mentor to provide guidance, correction and lead you as you grow closer to him.

However, because we live in a fallen world, there are also those among us who for several reasons, speak as if what they share is directly from God, and it is not.

In scripture, there is a story that comes to mind about an Old Prophet and a new Prophet (1 Kings 13). The lesson from this story is that when you hear from God, to trust what he says and heed his instruction, regardless of what it may look like or what may seem more reasonable. The new Prophet heeded the advice of the old Prophet, and it costed him his life, literally. Be discerning of the guidance you receive. Godly counsel and prophecy are two particularly useful ways that God speaks, when not abused. However, the counsel or prophecy you receive should always lead you back to God and never away from him or his word.

Pro tip:

Write down any prophetic word or counsel you receive. Reflect on it and what thoughts/emotions come up

Discernment tip:

The word says, *"By their fruit you will recognize them"* (Matthew 7:16). Pay close attention to the fruit in the life of the person advising you— whether through counsel or prophecy. Do you see evidence of spiritual maturity, integrity, and growth? Is there fruit in their family, relationships, health, or the work of their hands? These markers serve as significant clues about the spiritual competence and trustworthiness of their words.

<u>Spiritual gifts never trump character development.</u>

Take heed.

Reflective Question:

Think of a time when someone provided counsel or shared a prophetic word. How did it affect you?

Looking back, can you see if it aligned with God's word?

Key 7

Peace vs. Pressure: God doesn't Manipulate

Anchor Scripture:

"You will keep in perfect peace those whose minds are steadfast, because they trust in you."

Isaiah 26:3 (NIV)

Key Point: God leads his children through peace, not pressure. His voice is never manipulative, rushed, or forceful.

Teaching:

One thing I've learned is that God—and his Holy Spirit—are gentlemen. He doesn't barge into our lives. In 1 Kings 19:11–12, Elijah encounters the Lord not in the wind, earthquake, or fire, but in a *gentle whisper*. That whisper reveals his character.

He doesn't force us or manipulate us

He nudges

He convicts

He sends repetitive messages, dreams, and counsel

But ultimately, he gives us free will. This is the inherent ability to decide whether we will (or will not) heed what God is showing us. It's our choice.

When you face a decision, one of the greatest indicators of God's leading is the presence of peace. This is more than surface-level calm—it's a Spirit-deep assurance that steadies your heart. Peace allows you to rest, to sleep, to move forward without regret. On the other hand, pressure often shows up as anxiety, confusion, or a sense of being rushed into something prematurely. That's not God.

Pressure pushes.

Peace leads.

When God is silent (see Key 5), we can still trust his character. He doesn't use fear tactics or manipulation. His leading will always align with his Word and his peace.

Pro tip:

If you feel hurried into deciding, pause. Pressure often comes with a countdown clock. God's leading, while sometimes urgent, will still carry clarity and peace.

Discernment tip:

When torn between options, ask yourself: *"Which choice allows me to rest in God's peace, and which one leaves me unsettled?"*

Let peace, not pressure, be your compass.

Reflective Question:

Do you notice patterns in how you respond when under pressure? How can you train yourself to pause and listen for God's whisper instead

The Ongoing Conversation
(Closing note)

My prayer is that this book encourages you to grow in hearing God's voice in your daily life.

If you once burned with passion in your spiritual walk but find yourself struggling now, may these pages help you rekindle the flame.

If you are new to walking with God, may this devotional be the spark that lights the fire.

No matter where you are in your journey, remember that consistency sustains the fire. Daily prayer, time in God's Word, and intentional worship will keep the flame alive.

Return to these devotionals whenever you need reminding. Revisit the key concepts. Reread the scriptures.

Take time to write out your reflections, whether on the pages provided here or in your own journal. As you look back, you'll begin to see your growth and trace the threads of God's hand weaving your story together.

Always document what he shows you.

Treasure the whispers.

The puzzle pieces of his guidance may not always make sense in the moment, but in time, you'll look back and see the picture he was forming all along.

The conversation with God never ends—this is just the beginning.

About the Author

Dr. Tarasha is a Therapist, Author, and Professor with a heart for helping women heal. While she works with a variety of populations, her passion lies in supporting women as they break free from the past, overcome shame, and step boldly into cycles of self-love and restoration.

Blending clinical insight with spiritual wisdom, Dr. Tarasha creates safe spaces—both in her writing and counseling—for her clients to unpack their pain, challenge limiting beliefs, and embrace healing.

Dr. Tarasha aims to bridge faith and mental health, helping clients and readers alike move forward with clarity, confidence, and compassion.

When not counseling, teaching or writing, Dr. Tarasha enjoys hiking, double dutch, long car rides and spending time with her daughter.

For readers seeking healing from heartbreak, shame, and self-worth struggles, her first book, "The Self-Love Commandments', is available on Amazon. QR code linked included below

The Self-Love Commandments:
A Woman's Guide to Healing, Freedom and Love

Website: www.drtarasha.com

www.ingramcontent.com/pod-product-compliance
Lightning Source LLC
Chambersburg PA
CBHW031443120626
46545CB00006B/2533